ASPATORE
C-Level Business Intelligence™

Praise for Books, Business Intelligence Publications & Services

"What C-Level executives read to keep their edge and make pivotal business decisions. Timeless classics for indispensable knowledge." - Richard Costello, Manager-Corporate Marketing Communication, General Electric (NYSE: GE)

"True insight from the doers in the industry, as opposed to the critics on the sideline." - Steve Hanson, CEO, On Semiconductor (NASDAQ: ONNN)

"Unlike any other business books, Inside the Minds captures the essence, the deep-down thinking processes, of people who make things happen." - Martin Cooper, CEO, Arraycomm

"The only useful way to get so many good minds speaking on a complex topic." - Scott Bradner, Senior Technical Consultant, Harvard University

"Real advice from real experts that improves your game immediately." - Dan Woods, CTO, Capital Thinking

"Get real cutting edge industry insight from executives who are on the front lines." - Bob Gemmell, CEO, Digital Wireless

ASPATORE
C-Level Business Intelligence™

Publisher of Books, Business Intelligence Publications & Services

www.Aspatore.com

Aspatore is the world's largest and most exclusive publisher of C-Level executives (CEO, CFO, CTO, CMO, Partner) from the world's most respected companies. Aspatore annually publishes C-Level executives from over half the Global 500, top 250 professional services firms, law firms (MPs/Chairs), and other leading companies of all sizes in books, briefs, reports, articles and other publications. By focusing on publishing only C-Level executives, Aspatore provides professionals of all levels with proven business intelligence from industry insiders, rather than relying on the knowledge of unknown authors and analysts. Aspatore publishes an innovative line of business intelligence resources including Inside the Minds, Bigwig Briefs, ExecRecs, Business Travel Bible, Brainstormers, The C-Level Test, and Aspatore Business Reviews, in addition to other best selling business books, briefs and essays. Aspatore also provides an array of business services including The C-Level Library, PIA Reports, ExecEnablers, and The C-Level Review, as well as outsourced business library and researching capabilities. Aspatore focuses on traditional print publishing and providing business intelligence services, while our portfolio companies, Corporate Publishing Group (B2B writing & editing) and Aspatore Stores and Seminars focus on developing areas within the business and publishing worlds.

BIGWIG BRIEFS TEST PREP:
THE SERIES 7 EXAM

Real World Intelligence, Strategies & Experience From
Industry Experts to Prepare You for Everything the
Classroom and Textbooks Won't Teach You

ASPATORE
C-Level Business Intelligence™

Published by Aspatore Books, Inc.
For information on bulk orders, sponsorship opportunities or any other questions please email store@aspatore.com. For corrections, company/title up l dates, comments or any other inquiries please email info@aspatore.com.

First Printing, 2002
10 9 8 7 6 5 4 3 2 1

ISBN 1-58762-210-6

Edited By Laurie Mingolelli

Cover design by Rachel Kashon, Kara Yates, Ian Mazie

Material in this book is for educational purposes only. This book is sold with the understanding that neither any of the interviewees or the publisher is engaged in rendering legal, accounting, investment, or any other professional service.

This book is printed on acid free paper.

Special thanks also to: Ted Juliano, Tracy Carbone, and Rinad Beidas

The views expressed by the individuals in this book do not necessarily reflect the views shared by the companies they are employed by (or the companies mentioned in this book). The companies referenced may not be the same company that the individual works for since the publishing of this book.

The views expressed by the endorsements on the cover and in this book are from the book the original content appeared in and do not necessarily reflect the views shared by the companies they are employed by.

BIGWIG BRIEFS TEST PREP:
The Series 7 Exam

CONTENTS

BIGWIG BRIEFS TEST PREP:
THE SERIES 7 EXAM

How To Use This Book

Bigwig Briefs Test Prep: The Series 7 Exam features selections of condensed business intelligence from top industry insiders and is the best way for emerging business professionals to learn to think, analyze, and respond to situations they will confront in the workplace. The purpose of this book is not to devise the quickest way to answer a Series 7 options problem. Our strategy is geared towards the long-term, not the multiple choice quick-fix. We don't tell you how to fill in the dots and mark the grids; that you can find in a classroom or other books. Rather, we try to guide you towards assuming the mindset of the industry's most elite and successful professionals. If you learn to think like a stockbroker and approach decision-making firmly rooted in this mindset, you greatly increase your chances of having success on your Series 7 Exam, especially in answering the difficult questions that are impossible to study for. The authors in this book know what it takes to succeed; now you'll know their secrets, too. Use this information to get an edge and enable yourself to think like a stockbroker when taking the Series 7 Exam.

Scott Opsal, Invista Capital Management, LLC, Senior Vice President, Chief Technology Officer

A CTO's Practical Investing Tips: A Guide to Knowing When to Pull the Trigger

My personal approach to investing follows the classical lines of realizing when an asset is selling for a price lower than its fair value. I hesitate to use the words "value investor," because some people think value means just low P/E or low price to book. Value is actually defined as buying an asset for less than its worth. When I am investing I first analyze the long-term prospect of an asset, whether it is stock, bond, or real estate. Investing means understanding the asset's worth in a long-term, fair-market value and then trying to understand if it's mispriced in the short run and, if so, why. If an investor can identify a short-run pricing gap compared to fair value that is temporary or not justified, he or she should move in and buy that asset. I probably fit the mold of what is classically thought of as a value player, someone who looks at the long-term worth of an asset and buys it at a temporarily discounted price.

The art of investing has a couple of components that are not financial or mathematical at all. First, investing takes a lot of creative thinking. Whether you are a value investor, a growth investor, or a fixed-income specialist, you need to be a creative thinker. Most of the time, assets are fairly priced; the markets are pretty efficient – that is, markets price assets at values somewhat close to their fair economic value. If an asset is fairly or efficiently priced, the investor can expect to earn a fair rate of return on his investment but should not expect to earn an exceptional rate of return. If you think you have found an investment that is mispriced, you should stop and ask, "What can I see here that other people don't see? Why do I think this asset is mispriced?" And that question is usually not answered by poring over more financial statements than the other guy or running more computer models. It's more about looking at relationships.

Investing is all about making a comparative decision. Most investors are not deciding whether or not they should buy stock A. They are asking whether they should buy A or B, because they have assets to invest and want to put them to work. So it's the comparative decision. Because the market has already determined the price of each asset, an investor needs to be creative in looking for situations where two assets that should be influenced by the same factor are actually priced very differently. That goes back to the ability to recognize patterns and shifts differently than other people.

The second part of the art of investing involves risk analysis – not in the quantitative sense, but more in understanding when the odds are in your favor. This is true for whatever type of investor you are. One of the most important aspects of making good investments is to know when the odds are stacked in your favor, and the more biased, or "unfair," the odds seem to be tilted in your favor, the better. In the stock market you have the opportunity to buy 5,000 or 10,000 different stocks. In the bond market you have different credits and different durations. In both markets you have a multitude of economic scenarios, and you have to make a decision.

In looking at investors who succeed year in and year out, I think what differentiates them the most is that they can consistently identify conditions in which the odds are highly in their favor; their determination proves correct, and they are paid off. There's really no way to run it through a quantitative model or a screen or anything like that to decide the odds – it's strictly a judgment call. Perhaps the most important aspect of the art of investing is understanding the odds and pulling the trigger only when the odds are really on your side.

Golden Rules of Investing: What You Need to Know to Get Where You Want to Be Financially

The most important rule of investing is to have a process that will either work well or at least keep you above water in most conditions. The second rule is to understand that markets and stocks cycle up and down.

Inherent in the free market system, or capitalist system, is that the system will act to remove imbalances in the market. Over time, when things are really good, the system will slow it down and bring them back to normal. Whether the economy is booming or in a recession, understand the market will cycle back toward its normal state, which for us is a growth rate of maybe 3 percent, with the GDP maybe little higher. A free market never remains in an excess position or a deficit position too long.

The third important rule of investing is to be realistic. If you're in a recession, being realistic means, first of all, you don't know when the bottom is going to happen. The second thing you have to be realistic about is what your rate of returns can be in a down market. For example, to be realistic in a market such as the one we experienced from the start of 2000 to the start of 2001 means anyone who made more than 5 percent on their total portfolio did a good job: They lost money in stocks; they could have made money in bonds; and real estate had a good return. In a situation such as the 1990s, when earnings were rising, margins were rising, interest rates were falling, the economy was growing, and you had that once-in-every-20-years extra boost from the Internet and wireless build-out, your goal needs to be significantly higher.

The fourth crucial aspect of investing is being aware of taxes. I have done a lot of research on taxable investing, and I have managed taxable accounts. What I have learned through research and experience is that the amount of value you can add by properly managing your taxes, in my opinion, is just as significant as the amount of money you can make doing good research and analysis. In a stock portfolio I think you can add 200 basis points a year (or more) of return by managing your taxes well, which is about the same as the return a good investor can earn in large cap stocks.

The biggest key to managing your taxes involves a process called harvesting the capital losses. It is important to understand that market volatility actually is an advantage to a taxable investor. If you buy a stock today that you like and it goes down 20 percent, you should seriously consider taking that loss and reinvesting your money into a similar asset, maybe staying within the same industry but with a different company. Harvesting, or capturing, that loss gives you the flexibility to sell a winner when it's time to sell and pay no net capital gains taxes. By managing your taxes, and particularly by harvesting losses that are available in your portfolio, this tactic can be a huge windfall on top of your good research and good investment decisions. A taxable investor who properly measures their return on an after-tax basis can make almost as much money on their tax decisions as they can on their investment decisions. And certainly all the vehicles, such as 401(k)s and IRAs, that let you compound your returns on a pretax basis are absolutely part of the strategy.

Forecasting Market Direction

Knowing the basic principles of investing without taking into account the market's unpredictability can prove costly. When a person asks where the market is heading, an investor sees a probability question: What's the likelihood of the market going up or down? Or what forces would cause it to go up or down? As a fundamental investor, you look at valuation and earnings as the most important things. Valuation basically means examining the relationship between stocks and bonds and the relationship between stocks and other sectors of the stock market. In general, it's important to understand whether stocks or bonds are correctly priced, because it's not really a yes-no call; it's an either-or call.

The direction of the stock market is quite often influenced by the opportunity on the other side of the table. For example, when stocks sold off rapidly in the fall of 1987, I think it was driven by the realization that bonds had a higher expected long-run return than stocks had, and people reacted to that. I think the bull market of most of the 1990s was a reflection of interest rates consistently falling, and that made stocks an increasingly more attractive option. If bonds yield only 5 percent or 6 percent, stocks have a very easy hurdle to beat. One of the critical issues is the relationship between stocks and alternative assets because, at the end of the day, that's really going to drive the marginal cash flow into the market.

The second thing to watch when forecasting the market is earnings. When all is said and done, a company's stock is priced on earnings. So one of the key questions today is whether it's going to be a short or long-lasting trough for earnings. Furthermore, bull and bear markets are almost always driven by either interest rates or earning swings. Events such as a war or political situations usually don't have a long-term impact.

To help you understand the market's inclination, the thing to look for is relative strength on news flow. If the market doesn't go down when bad news hits, it tells you the preferred direction is up. On the other hand, if the market won't rise anymore on good news, the preferred direction is down. When calling turns in the market, it's important to understand which direction investor sentiment wants the market to go. It might sound silly that investors would ever want it to go down, but in fact when people realize stocks are pricey and the environment is getting worse, they want to get out. I do think it works in both directions.

Adapting Investment Strategies to Survive in Turbulent Markets

An investor's style should change in several ways in a turbulent market. First, a good investor becomes a more active decision-maker. In a turbulent market, the reason the market is moving up or down is that something is changing in the current situation or, more probably, in expectations for the future. As a result, an investor has more of these relationships to understand and reconsider in a period of great flux. For example, the market could move 10 percent or more in just a week, forcing the investor to refigure all those relationships. Now, this does not mean you trade more often; you're just offered decisions to make more often, and that becomes an extra opportunity and an extra burden.

The second aspect of an investor's approach that changes is the evaluation of the fair value of an asset. In turbulent conditions, it's not quite as clear whether the long-term value has or hasn't changed. For example, in a bear market for an investor like me to buy an asset I think is mispriced, I also have had to decide that its long-term value has not eroded and that the bear market is not correctly pricing the asset. When you have a turbulent market the turbulence comes from the uncertainty about the future, which means there's uncertainty about what assets are really worth. In effect, the good investor has to raise his or her standard of decision making to be able to confidently say, "I really still believe this company is undervalued or this bond is too cheap." In a turbulent market an investor is less certain of the foundation or fixed point of reference in terms of value.

The third important thing in a turbulent market is to be much more aware of other investors' sentiment in the market. When the market is turbulent and you sense uncertainty, people aren't able to use their traditional processes of discounted cash flow or P/E measures or any other technique they relied upon in the past. If those models aren't working because the market is moving too quickly, they have to rely on something else, and that's usually sentiment.

Even though I prefer to invest based on economic decision making, a successful investor can't ignore feelings in a turbulent market, because they probably will be the main driver in the short run. More to the point, if you're on the wrong side of sentiment you can get beaten up fast, even if you're right in the long run. Becoming much more aware of sentiment, the investor factors it more heavily into his or her decision when the market is moving rapidly in either direction.

Recently this has occurred on both sides. In the technology growth stock boom of 1999 and early-2000 – whether or not you thought those stocks were a good deal – sentiment was clearly on the upside, and you had to consider that. Now, within the past year you have had sentiment on the downside, and you have had to consider that, as well. Although it is not really an economic term or a financial factor to consider, in markets that are volatile and moving you have to judge sentiment correctly, or all of your other work could be blown away by that one issue.

Fundamental and Technical Analyses Made Simple

On the technical side of studying stocks and investments, there is very little economic analysis. A good investor watches the relative strength of companies and relative strengths of industries. It's more a measure of where these companies have been and what the market and investors have decided about these companies, rather than where they are going. In my opinion technical analysis doesn't personally tell me much about the future. But I do know that quite often swings in the market are self-correcting. Groups of companies tend to cycle up and down. When one group outperforms another, it has become more highly valued because more of its good news has been taken into account, and it has a more optimistic outlook. Once a stock has outperformed long enough, it becomes "priced for perfection," meaning the market has attributed a great deal of good news to the stock. From that point the odds generally favor the next piece of news or the next development being bad, and that group is unlikely to continue to go up indefinitely. Similarly, the groups of stocks that have underperformed have done so because of a piece of bad news. The lower it goes, the higher the odds become that it's going to rebound and come back.

Beyond the news flow issue, stock prices are always influenced by their fair economic value. Although stocks generally do not trade at their fair value, their price action is certainly influenced by that. A stock that has been outperforming for some time has likely risen well above fair value, and that gap is likely to narrow in the future. Similarly, stock that has underperformed for some time has likely fallen well below fair value, and going forward that relationship will act to pull the price back up a bit. As an investor, when you look at technical analysis, you really see where things have been recently to tell you how much of the good or bad news has already been priced into the asset, and how far the stock might have drifted from its fair value.

On the fundamental side, a good investor can look at three different components of company analysis. The first thing is to understand a company's business, its business strategy, and its competitive position. This involves understanding a company's market share, its competition, its growth rate in end-user demand, and its ability to defend its margins, because that's what really helps you decide what the long-term value of the asset is. The more a company grows and the more it's able to defend its growth rate, its market share, and its margins, then the more it's worth.

The second piece of analysis involves valuation. In valuation analysis, an investor looks at two things. One is the free cash flow measure, which tells the investor how much value is left for the stockholders after a company takes in its revenue, pays its expenses, and reinvests in its capital and its equipment. It's important to compare the free cash flow to the current stock price. By doing so, an investor determines the internal rate of return of the stock; that is, the rate of return the company's stockholders as a group will earn from being owners of the business. In bonds, yield to maturity is the valuation measure that compares future cash flows (coupons) with current price. The same measure can be calculated for a stock.

I also look at relative valuation. For any company I am considering, I identify a handful of peers in the industry and examine how they are valued relative to each other. Investing is a comparative decision question – a person must decide how interesting a company is compared to the others. If a relative peer group valuation analysis turns up a more interesting company than the one you started with, the investor can switch his focus. At the end of the day investors basically want to believe they have an asset that has a good rate of return on its own and that there isn't another similar asset that is an even better deal. If you can answer those two questions, you have resolved the valuation piece.

The third thing to look at in a fundamental company analysis is timeliness. Considering timeliness is making a judgment as to whether today is the right day to get into that asset. For me, that's a much tougher question to answer than whether it's a good investment. A lot of discounted-price or value investors are so early on an asset that they can appear to be wrong because they give up too much going down before the stock turns around. So timeliness is important.

With timeliness, you look at trends in earnings and margins, and estimate revisions and earning surprises to get a true sense of the business momentum of the company. Momentum is discussed a lot in the stock market, mostly on a price momentum basis. It's a chart-reading issue of how fast and how consistently a stock's price is rising. I find little value here, but there is much more value in watching business, or fundamental, momentum.

When looking at business momentum, you look at the margins of business to see if it is doing better than it was in prior periods, or whether the sales are growing a little faster. These will also create improving earnings estimates and rising analyst rankings, which are two other important measures of business momentum. These are the types of things that will change an investor's sentiment, which in effect is what timeliness is trying to look at. You have to be able to say not only that you have an asset that is undervalued today, but you also have a reason to believe the business is steadily improving and investors are going to warm up to the asset rather than cool off on it in the short run. The biggest danger in being a long-term fundamental investor is being too early and losing too much on the way down.

The Importance of Discipline in the Stock Market

Discipline, or having a process and sticking to it, is another trait almost every successful long-run investor has. Self-enforced discipline comes from will power and confidence and involves several levels. First, each investor has to understand his or her own philosophy and process. Are you a value player? Are you growth? Are you short- or long-term? You need to understand yourself and not try to employ someone else's process, because the first time another's process doesn't work you'll blame the other person's process and say it was a dumb idea. For those of you who don't know your own personal investment beliefs, there have been many good investment books written over the years. I encourage my staff to read as many as they can. I encourage the average investor to read as many as they can and to figure out which line of thinking they believe feels right to them. Although there are many ways to make money in stocks, you have to pick one and stick with it. That's the first level of discipline.

At the second level of discipline, you use that process on every position that you take. If you buy a few stocks using your basic process, and then buy a stock because of a good tip or something you think is happening in the market, you place yourself at risk both financially and emotionally. As soon as you deviate from your process and the stock goes down, not only do you lose money but you also kick yourself for knowing better. As soon as your self-confidence is shaken, your risk goes up of making bad decisions going forward because you are now gun-shy. Most good processes have been proved to work *over time* if followed consistently and carefully. One thing I have never seen is a good investor who is able to consistently change his or her process at the right time and make it work. So the second level of discipline is to stick to your process for every decision.

At the third level of discipline, you understand that not every process will work in every stage of a market cycle or in every time period. But a good process should at least allow you to hold your ground in periods when it is somewhat out of favor. If there's a wild-growth mania, as we saw in 1999, a value-based player will not make the most money he can, but that's okay. It's important to understand it's okay because every good process has days when it won't work, but it has more days when it will work.

Having a process you believe in is a huge boost of confidence I think you need to have. A process enables you to say, "I may be wrong today, but I know why I bought the stock. I believe on average my process will work, and that's all I need to know. I don't need dwell on it anymore."

Timing: When to Get In, When to Get Out

Deciding when it's time to get in or out of a position is a comparative decision. It's looking at my best idea that I don't own versus the least interesting idea that I do own. Sometimes, getting in or out of a position might be driven by the other stocks you want to buy in place of the one you already own. Assuming an investor has a stock that popped up and looks interesting, you like the story; the point of pulling the trigger depends on the timeliness.

For example, if the news flow going forward is neutral or positive – and I don't think it will be negative – that will be a trigger to get in. Then I'll also look at the relative strength – whether the stock has already started to run or not. If a stock has started to run, I'll generally get in at a partial weighting from what I think my total position will be. Maybe I'll buy in at a half weighting on the basis that if it has run a little, it might give some back, and I can pick up a little more at the bottom. If it looks as though it has bottomed out and set a price level, then I'll go ahead and buy a full position. Building a position in a new stock can be thought of in much the same way as the dollar cost averaging approach that people use with a stock or a fund. If the moon and the stars are lined up perfectly for this stock, I am going to get in now, but if I think there is a chance the news flow will turn bad, I'll leave a little powder dry and get in a little more later. Most often you'll get a chance to buy in at a later date.

A lot of investors like to do what they can to avoid the risk of regret. Regret is saying in hindsight that you wish you had done something different or at a different time. If you buy a partial position, you obviously leave yourself a mental out to say, "If it goes down, I have room to buy a little more at a better price, and if it goes up, at least I got a partial position before it moved on me." It's like golf pros who, every time they miss a putt, blame a spike mark or a bump on the green. Investors need the same mental trick to avoid consistently thinking they may not have called a stock exactly right. A dollar cost average approach really minimizes your risk of regret and helps you avoid losing sleep because you think you did the wrong thing. And again, you have to balance it with not being too much of a chicken.

Getting out is about as tough as or tougher than getting in. Once you're in, you have not only the analytical capital invested, but you also have invested your personal capital of being wrong. As a result, people don't like to sell.

The art of investing is making good decisions when the odds are in your favor. The best process is to actually decide at the time you buy a stock what it will take to sell it; that is, it's time to sell the stock when the reasons you bought it no longer exist or are no longer true. If the condition under which I bought has now happened, I usually will go ahead and sell it. If you simply wait to decide on the spot whether to sell, you will be influenced by too many short-term events: If the stock price is running, you will say you'll hold it for one more dollar, which is not a reasonable, well-thought-out decision to make. If it's a loss, you might say it will come back if you wait long enough. Those are not analytical risk-analysis calls; those are gut feelings. On a day-to-day basis, people who watch the market will have more gut-feel decisions that they want to make than sound, rational decisions they should make. The best way to make any call is to decide up front what it will take to sell.

Howard Weiss, Bank of America,
Senior Vice President

A Ten-Point Program for Successful Investing

Over the years much science and mathematics have grown around the practice of investing. On the other hand, there is also a considerable "art" to successful investing. The trick is to effectively weave the "art" and "science" together into an overall, long-term plan that can operate in both up and down markets. To accomplish that I have generally followed this 10-point program when advising wealthy families and individuals:

1. Establish goals.
2. Define risks.
3. Develop asset class strategies.
4. Establish asset allocation targets.
5. Construct the actual investment portfolio, selecting the appropriate securities, vehicles, and/or managers.
6. Manage your stock portfolio through a disciplined stock selection approach.
7. Hedge specific portfolio risks.

8. Manage tax position.
9. Evaluate portfolio performance.
10. Rebalance the portfolio.

1. Establishing Investment Goals

The first step in the process is to define your investment objectives and profile your needs. You will want to consider the following elements:

❏ What are your income needs after tax?
❏ How do you profile your risk tolerance?
❏ What is your time horizon? This will be different for each investment pool. For instance, educational funds will correspond to your children's ages and may have a different time horizon from your personal portfolio or retirement funds.
❏ What is your need for liquidity? This involves planning for major expenditures and structuring your portfolio to accommodate your expected cash withdrawal rates. Pure liquidity should include cash reserves and income, as well as assets you can sell at no loss.

❏ How much of your portfolio must be marketable? A marketable security is one you can convert to cash at today's market value, even if you are selling at a loss.

❏ What is your tax situation? What is your income tax bracket, and do you have any loss carry-forwards that can be used? Do you have alternative minimum tax problems?

❏ Finally, what are your growth expectations? Are your assets and income adequate to meet your needs? To what degree do your assets need to grow to meet your lifestyle needs?

2. Defining Investment Risks

The first step in handling risk is to understand the various types of investment risk. Here are some of the major ones:

❏ *Reinvestment risk* is associated with the redeployment of maturing bonds and future cash flows. The implication is that you may not wish to have too many bond maturities in any one year.

❏ *Inflation, or purchasing power, risk* is associated with changes in the price levels of goods and services.

Investors will want to achieve returns that exceed the increase in inflation over the years.

❏ *Credit risk* is associated with a company's uncertainty in earnings and sometimes its ability to survive.

❏ *Currency risk* relates to changes in the exchange rate between the dollar and foreign currencies. This sometimes has an impact on the earnings and, ultimately, the stock prices of multinational companies.

❏ *Event risk* is associated with a nonfinancial event hitting a company. Examples include a governmental action, such as a Justice Department monopoly suit or a Food & Drug Administration order.

❏ *Market risk* is the risk associated with the rise and fall of the stock market and its ramifications to the economy.

❏ *Common-factor risk* is the specific risk inherent with securities that have similar attributes. Examples include high or low P/E stocks, small cap stocks, cyclical stocks, and defensive stocks. During certain business conditions, stocks with these similar attributes may move in tandem.

3. Establishing Asset Class Strategies

Academic studies have shown asset allocation is the single largest determinant of performance. Accordingly, many will argue that asset allocation decisions are the most important decisions you will make as an investor. Different asset classes outperform at different times, and over the past 16 years no single asset class has consistently been the top performer. Moreover, asset classes that are on top one year are suddenly found on the bottom the following year, and vice versa.

Arriving at your asset mix is a multistage process. It begins with identifying the range of asset classes you feel are essential to help reach your income and growth objectives and, at the same time, are consistent with your risk parameters. Next, you need to clearly understand the specific return and risk profile of each asset class. You then determine how to arrange each asset class within your portfolio. We will consider each phase.

When identifying asset classes, I advise clients to consider a wide range of traditional asset classes, and for wealthy clients, I also advise that they consider a range of alternative investments where appropriate. Here is a brief listing of the various asset classes.

Cash Equivalents
Commercial paper
U.S. T-bills & agcy notes
Auction rate municipals
Municipal notes

Fixed Income
Domestic taxable bonds
Municipal bonds
International bonds
High-yield bonds

Equities
Large cap stocks
Small/mid cap stocks
International stocks
Emerging market stocks

Alternative strategies
Private equities
Exchange funds
Real estate
Hedge funds

Hedge funds represent a unique type of asset class and have a range of strategies themselves. Here are some of them.

Diversified Strategies
Fund of funds
Managed futures
(CTA) index

Market Strategies
Equity hedge
Short selling
Emerging markets

Hedge fund index	Fixed income high-yield
Global markets	**Arbitrage strategies**
Macro	Market neutral
Market timing	Convertible arbitrage
Discretionary CTA	Event-driven
Trend-followers CTA	Distressed securities

I advise clients to understand how each asset class contributes to the performance, as well as the risk, of the portfolio. Here is a brief synopsis of some of the major asset classes I work with and the role they play in a portfolio:

Cash equivalents represent the liquidity portion of your portfolio. Generally, this segment contains money market funds, treasury bills, certificates of deposit, and commercial paper. Investments are either immediate cash *(e.g.,* money market funds), or they mature within 12 months.

Fixed income instruments are essentially debt securities of the U.S. government and agencies, corporations, states, and municipalities. They provide the greatest part of a portfolio's income. While the long-term expected return of bonds is measurably lower than its equity counterparts, the long-term volatility of bonds is also much lower. There are also two special types of fixed income that can play a useful role in one's portfolio:

High-yield bonds are generally debt obligations of corporations with a credit rating of BB or lower. They carry a higher yield to compensate for the increased credit risk. In many ways they act in concert with the stock market. During good economic times, their yield spread to higher quality debt narrows, while during bad economic times, their yield spread widens.

Convertible bonds and convertible preferred stocks are securities issued by corporations and can be converted into corresponding stock at a predetermined price level. They are attractive investments during difficult markets because they provide yield support to a stock while at the same time enabling the investor to participate on the upside if the stock rises.

Large-capitalization equities represent stocks of large publicly traded companies whose market capitalization exceeds $10 billion. These are generally mature companies that are actively followed by securities analysts. They form the cornerstone of any equity component of a portfolio, as there will be many years when this asset class outperforms other asset classes. For example, over the past 16 years, either large cap growth or large cap value ranked among the top three performing asset classes. The challenge for the investor is to determine how to play the large cap market between value and growth investing. I will comment on a suggested strategy.

Mid cap equities represent stocks of medium-size publicly traded companies whose market capitalization ranges between $1 billion and $10 billion. Most companies are mature, but some are not, and this segment is moderately covered by Wall Street analysts. They are somewhat less liquid than large capitalization stocks. I regularly recommend this asset class, as it provides access to many up-and-coming growth companies that have emerged from the risks of the start-up phase. They perform very well after a recession and provide decent returns during up markets.

Small cap equities represent stocks of small-size publicly traded companies whose market capitalization falls below $1 billion. Generally, these companies are not widely followed by Wall Street analysts and are less liquid than large or mid-cap stocks. Over the long term small cap stocks have provided greater returns than large cap stocks but with much greater volatility. Like mid-cap stocks, these stocks tend to do well out of a recession and do reasonably well during the growth periods of an up market. On the other hand, they get hit during recessionary times, as you would expect.

International equities represent ownership of internationally domiciled companies that are traded on stock exchanges of developed countries. I generally recommend an allocation to this sector, because many of the world's major corporations are now non-U.S. and many foreign economies have shown attractive growth rates over the years. Also, many U.S. companies have global ties. From a portfolio standpoint, international equities offer attractive diversification opportunities due to their low correlation to domestic equities.

Private equity is the first of my alternative strategies. This asset class includes investments in private companies. Among these investments are venture capital, leveraged buy-outs, recapitalizations, reorganizations, restructurings, privatizations, and spin-offs. Private equity is available only to "qualified investors" who have a minimum of $5 million in securities they can invest. Private equity investing, as you might expect, requires a long-term commitment, as it has limited liquidity. Nevertheless, it can be a rewarding investment experience, and I recommend it to some of my clients, especially those who have owned private companies of their own.

Real estate can also be an important long-term asset for larger portfolios, as it offers some important benefits. As a diversification play, it has a low correlation with stocks and bonds. Commercial real estate with long-term leases will not only provide a good income source, but also have low principal volatility and offer a reasonable chance for capital appreciation over the long term. Most investors expect real estate to earn a total rate of return between bonds and stock. There are risks, however, including tenant default, inability to rent some of the properties, and deteriorating locations.

Hedge funds are the most intriguing asset class. Established as private investment partnerships, hedge funds operate under limited regulations and will generally invest in futures, commodities, options, currencies, and stock market indexes, in addition to stocks and bonds. They also frequently employ leverage and sell securities short. There are a variety of hedge fund strategies, some of which I referred to earlier. On the other hand, there are two major styles:

Arbitrage, or market neutral, involves investing in offsetting long and short equity positions in the same sectors. Market risk is greatly reduced, and leverage may be employed. Correlation to the general equity market is low.

Multistrategy involves investing in the broader market, including arbitrage, but also including directional strategies.

Hedge funds also entail a fair amount of risk and drawbacks. Among those are tax inefficiency, limited liquidity, limited transparency, short-selling, leverage, and no registration under the Investment Company Act of 1940. Finally, hedge funds are generally restricted to accredited investors and qualified purchasers who have more than $5 million of assets they can invest. I generally recommend hedge funds to wealthy individuals because of their low correlation to other asset classes. Moreover, certain hedge fund structures can provide positive returns in down markets. Discussing hedge funds further is beyond the scope of this chapter, and you should consult your financial advisor before purchasing these types of investments.

4. Establishing Asset Allocation Targets

Once you identify the specific asset classes to invest in, the next step is to figure out how to allocate them within the portfolio. Your investment objectives and risk profile will provide meaningful inputs to this process, and two statistical measures should provide an important backdrop: 1) the expected return and; 2) the expected risk, as measured by the standard deviation. The expected return of a portfolio is partially based on the expected returns of the asset classes that make up the portfolio. The expected return of an asset class is predominately based on historical results but may also include a component for anticipated changes in the future. The standard deviation measures the variability of investment returns. One standard deviation explains 68 percent of the return, and two standard deviations generally explain 95 percent of the return. For example, if an asset class has an expected return of 10 percent and a standard deviation of 9 percent, you would expect that 68 percent of the time, the return would fall between 1 percent and 19 percent.

5. Constructing Your Portfolio

The final step in setting asset allocation targets is to arrange the asset classes into a portfolio in the most efficient way to obtain the most attractive return/risk trade-off. Before doing so, there is one additional statistical measure of importance. This is the "correlation coefficient," which measures the sensitivity of returns of one asset class to the returns of another. A highly positive correlation (near 1.0) indicates a direct relationship, while a negative correlation (near -1.0) indicates an inverse relationship between the asset classes. On the other hand, a correlation factor near zero means a specific asset class has little sensitivity to the movement of the other.

Correlation plays a major role in determining a portfolio's overall expected return. For example, two asset classes could each carry a high level of risk, but if they do not move in tandem, then each can offset the volatility of the other. Again, as a way of illustration, consider the following example of the estimated correlation of certain asset classes in relation to large cap equities, as measured by the S&P 500 Index.

Index	Correlation Factor
S&P 500	1.000
Russell Mid Cap	0.934
Russell 2000 (Small Cap)	0.795
MSCI EAFE (International)	0.517
LB Aggregate Bond	0.331
U.S. T-Bill (Cash)	-0.019
Hedge Funds	0.507

At this point you are ready to determine your actual portfolio mix. I regularly advise clients to use some form of portfolio optimizer to establish a statistical basis for this decision. A portfolio optimizer is essentially a computerized program that combines three inputs – expected returns of each asset class, their standard deviations, and estimates of their cross-correlation – to arrive at the "efficient frontier" portfolio. The efficient frontier represents the theoretical set of portfolios that provide the highest rate of expected return for each level of expected risk. By using these techniques, you can statistically design portfolios that offer "the most bang for your buck," meaning the best return for the level of risk you take.

After establishing asset allocation targets, you begin the challenging task of selecting the appropriate securities, investment vehicles, and managers for each asset class. For most asset classes, there are a variety of investment forms. Some require minimum investments, so the options could narrow for certain investors who either cannot or will not commit the necessary funds. I will discuss these forms within the context of each asset class.

Cash equivalents are most efficiently managed through money market mutual funds. However, during a rising rate environment, you may wish to buy short-term CDs, Treasury Bills, or tax-free variable rate demand notes, as they will reflect current interest rates, while money market mutual funds will have some "older securities" at lower rates.

Bond portfolios can be managed via mutual funds or in a separate portfolio of individual securities. Bonds can also be professionally managed by a money manager. If you use funds, it is important to understand the average maturity objective of each one, as well as their taxability and general credit quality. For a separately managed portfolio, I generally recommend that clients ladder the maturities to reduce the reinvestment risk and always be in a position to take advantage of rising rates.

Large cap stock portfolios can take the form of mutual funds or a separately managed portfolio. There are many elements to mutual fund investing in this asset class; here are some of them:

❏ Many funds will follow a specific style – either value, growth, or a combination. These styles will not always move together. I generally advise clients who use

❏ mutual funds in this class to diversify their assets among both growth and value managers. If you can pick the right funds, and each outperforms its peers, you should achieve strong long-term performance.

❏ Some mutual funds replicate the S&P 500 Index and are appropriately termed "index funds." These investments are sometimes favored by investors because of their greater performance predictability (versus the index), lower turnover, and lower tax liabilities. While I do not regularly recommend these instruments, if they are appropriate in certain client situations, I will use them.

❏ Annual turnover and, consequently, expected tax liabilities are critical when evaluating mutual funds. Additionally, it is important to distinguish between short-term and long-term gains because of the significant difference in those respective tax rates.

Mid and small cap stock portfolios can also take the form of mutual funds, much like their large cap counterparts.

Here again, I recommend either diversifying between value and growth investing or selecting funds that cover both disciplines. Where possible, I also suggest separate account management because of the tax issues. I do not recommend indexing this segment because there is substantial room for a portfolio manger to outperform the indices due to less complete information flow on these types of companies.

International stocks can be managed in separate portfolios, but it is costly to do so. So the most efficient vehicle is the mutual fund or, if available, a limited partnership. The partnership is more effective from a tax standpoint, since investors can maintain their own cost basis when they buy into the fund. They do not incur the built-in gains on the existing portfolio. Losses can also be passed on in many cases.

Real estate investments generally take the form of limited partnerships or real estate investment trusts (REITs). The REITs act, in many ways, like common stocks, and they trade on the national exchanges. For the lower dollar investments a REIT is just fine, while, for the investor who wants to make a significant commitment to real estate, certain limited partnerships are attractive.

Hedge fund investments can be accessed in two ways. First, you can try to buy a hedge fund directly. The issues in doing this, however, are that most funds have very high minimums, and they are sometimes closed to new investors. Also, you may have limited liquidity, and you do not get manager diversification. The second way to invest is through a fund of funds. I usually suggest this approach to clients because you have fewer problems with access; you receive diversification in styles; liquidity is somewhat better; and a professional manager conducts extensive due diligence and regularly monitors the underlying managers.

Private equity investments can take the form of a direct private investment in a company, purchase of a specific private equity fund, or purchase of a fund of funds. Here again, I tend to suggest the fund of funds route because of access, diversification, and professional oversight.

6. *Managing the Stock Portfolio*

While asset allocation may be the single most important determinant of performance, most investors still enjoy the action of picking individual stocks. Staying consistent with my approach to asset allocation, I also believe in a somewhat disciplined approach to stock selection and like to follow a three-point approach.

First, I do not believe in market timing, so whatever allocation you designate for large cap equities, for example, should be invested solely in that asset class. If your personal investment objectives change, and you wish to revise your asset mix accordingly, that is perfectly fine; however, I do not advise clients to try to out-guess or time the direction of the markets. At the same time, I believe there is considerable risk in aggressively overweighting or underweighting particular sectors of the market.

If you do not practice market timing and keep sector weightings tight, your margin of victory needs to come from stock selection. Accordingly, my objective is to hold the best companies within each sector. This means not just holding the hot stocks in the hot industries, but also investing in solid companies that might be in depressed or out-of-favor industries.

To arrive at the actual stocks to buy, I generally practice a relative value approach, with a twist. Essentially, I look at three levels of analysis.

At the top level I suggest companies be analyzed on the basis of those valuation measures pertinent to their industry and sector. I do not suggest they be absolute valuations but instead, be valuations relative to others in a firm's industry or relative to its own history. Here are some of these valuation measures:

❏ Relative Price Earnings Ratio
❏ Relative Price to Book Ratio
❏ Relative Price to Cash Flow
❏ Relative Return on Equity

During certain economic environments, it may not be easy to find attractive valuations. Particularly during a growth market, higher P/E stocks could perform much better than lower P/E stocks. Accordingly, if you find a particular sector, such as technology, lacks good opportunities, you should revert to certain earnings growth measures. Two of the more important ones are earnings momentum and earnings surprise.

Earnings momentum shows the acceleration of quarterly earnings. The theory is that if a company's business is on the upswing and its earnings are continually rising, the stock price will continue to advance in almost a direct fashion. The converse is true if a company's earnings are falling.

Earnings surprise measures how well a company meets its earnings forecasts. The theory here is that Wall Street analysts evaluate a stock on the basis of its expected earnings. If a company regularly comes in better than expected, then the stock is likely to pop and be afforded a higher valuation than a company that regularly disappoints analysts on its earnings.

Finally, there are still certain times when neither traditional valuation nor earnings growth measures will get you to companies you like. In these cases qualitative factors become far more important. Recessionary periods usually feature high or even negative P/E ratios and negative earnings growth rates. As a result I tend to look at companies with some of these characteristics or qualities:

❏ Strong management.
❏ Leading market share. I prefer market leaders, especially during weak economic times, as these companies are better able to weather the storm. They also tend to be the first out of the gate when conditions improve. Companies that are number two in many product lines may also be okay.
❏ Strong brands.
❏ Financial strength with less debt than others and relatively strong cash flow.
❏ Good cost structure, also enabling the firm to handle poor economic times better, as they do not have to sell as much to earn money and have better pricing power.
❏ Innovative product development.

Appropriate examples surround the Internet and technology industries, where stock prices collapsed in mid-2000.

Applying the above discipline takes you immediately to a consideration of the qualitative factors, since valuations are still high, and there is no earnings momentum yet. When this is the case, I tend to favor the strongest companies – those with strong managements, dominant market shares, strong capital bases, and well-recognized brands. At the end of the recovery some of the weaker companies may actually outperform if they survive; however, I am generally not willing to take the necessary risk in such battered industries. Moreover, as an industry recovery begins, the larger and stronger companies usually lead the way, so you may have time to pick up some of the secondary names later on.

As for the Internet and tech industry in general, even though these industries have significant overcapacity, and the stocks are way off their highs, the Internet has forever changed our business and personal lives and the way we communicate with each other. Consequently, this industry will not go away. It is just going through a down business cycle, and investors need to stay the course and keep participating in it. You may not want to risk capital in the weakest companies or in questionable start-ups, but you should not abandon some of the strong names, such as Intel, Dell, Cisco, Sun Microsystems, Oracle, and EMC, among others. If you are hesitant about some of these, you can always go to IBM.

7. *Hedge Specific Portfolio Risk*

Some investors will hold a concentrated position in a single stock. This may have occurred by selling a business for the stock of another company or just through sheer appreciation. In any event, large concentrations do carry the significant risk of deterioration in the fortunes of a single company. To deal with this type of risk there are a variety of techniques available today. I work with many clients to mitigate such risks and here are some of the techniques I may advise clients to use:

To provide substantial downside protection, investors can purchase a *put option*. This transaction gives the purchaser the right to sell the underlying stock at a predetermined price, called the "put stock price," at some future date. This option enables the investor to still participate fully in any appreciation. I advise clients to do this when they want to just cover their downside, but want to retain the full upside appreciation potential. This transaction does cost money in the form of a put premium paid by the investor to the seller of the put.

If an investor just wants to protect the current price level of a stock but wishes to do so at no cost, he or she can enter into a *costless collar* transaction. Here the investor purchases a put option with a strike price at or below the current stock price and combines it with the sale of a call option with a strike price above the current stock price. A call option gives the purchaser the right to buy the stock at a predetermined price in the future. He pays the seller a premium for this right. By establishing a collar, minimum and maximum prices are set around a stock. It can also be structured in a way that the premium received from the call option offsets the premium paid for the put option. I advise clients to consider this transaction when they wish to hedge a substantial part of their downside risk while retaining some upside appreciation.

Another way to diversify away from a concentrated position is to contribute your stock to an exchange fund. These vehicles are partnerships where "qualified investors" can contribute their stock into a fund as a tax-free exchange. These funds have termination dates and, at that time, investors can either receive their contributed stock back or receive a pro-rated share of the portfolio. You retain your original cost basis but have a diversified portfolio. I recommend this approach when clients want to move out of their stock and diversify but do not wish to incur a taxable event.

8. Managing Your Tax Position

While I never advise clients to let the "tax tail wag the dog," I do advocate efficient tax management of a portfolio. There are several strategies you can follow to gain optimal tax efficiency. Here are some of the common ones:

❑ Effectively manage short-term versus long-term capital gains. All things being equal, you should sell the asset

❏ that would result in a long-term versus short-term gain, as short-term gains are taxable at the higher ordinary rates.

❏ Harvest your losses, using them to offset gains elsewhere in your investment portfolio or business ventures.

❏ Judiciously employ year-end swaps in both your stock and bond portfolios.

9. Evaluating Portfolio Performance

Investments is a highly competitive game with winners and losers. This means investors need to establish a process for evaluating whether they are winning or losing. To accomplish this, you should evaluate the performance of each asset class against an appropriate market index, as well as against similar style managers.

While you might wish to evaluate your performance monthly or quarterly at least, you should not make significant changes in a fund or manager just because of their short-term relative performance. Generally, you should allow a mutual fund or professional manager at least three years or a full market cycle before judging their relative performance.

10. Rebalancing Your Portfolio.

Perhaps the most critical facet of investing is to know when to sell. Some investment experts tell you to sell when a company is just beginning to experience poor sales and earnings, but then it is usually too late. Others apply disciplines that suggest selling when a stock goes down by a certain percentage or dollar amount. On the flip side, certain experts suggest selling when a stock becomes overvalued, as measured by its price earnings ratio.

I am not sure there is any sure-fire formula for selling stocks or any class of investments. Consequently, I advise clients to employ a continuous top-down process for reducing overweighted asset classes and stock positions, and then rebalancing their portfolios. It is a relatively simple, but disciplined, program. The process begins at the asset allocation level. and reinvest. I usually advise a selective process in which you look for overvalued securities first. This way, you are addressing potential risks. Should valuation methods not result in the reductions needed, then you can use earnings growth and qualitative factors. Then, of course, if these also do not yield results, you can fall back on the pro-rata approach. The important point is that heavily overweighted asset classes should be cut back, and as a result, overweighed and possibly overvalued sectors and securities would be scaled back, as well.

Victoria Collins, The Keller Group Investment Management, Inc., Executive Vice President and Principal

As a Financial Advisor, Are You Truly Benefiting Your Clients?

When clients come into my office, they bring two financial portfolios. One includes their brokerage statements, tax returns, bank information, balance sheet, cash flow statement, insurance policies – documents we can lay out on the table and see, touch, and quantify. The other financial file is just as important, but far less visible. It can't be opened for review or spread out on the table. This portfolio holds the clients' hopes, fears, dreams, past experiences, style of managing, what they would like their money to accomplish for them. Unless we can integrate those two portfolios, no investment model or financial plan, no matter how well-designed, will work.

When the markets are going up, it's easy to for an advisor to look good. But when the markets perform as they did in 2000 and 2001, that's when we advisors really get tested.

Not only are our skills and abilities on trial, but also, and maybe more important, how well we communicate with our clients about what's happening in the markets.

As a client, you should expect your advisor to keep you posted on the markets and the economy and how these forces are affecting your investments. Your advisor should check with you from time to time to confirm your objectives. This open dialogue is important and helps ensure that your wishes are being carried out.

When I think about risk, it's interesting to note that during 1998 and 1999, I saw a significant increase in how comfortable clients *said* they felt with risk. What risk was and how to determine how much one should take never came up unless I brought it up. It's also interesting that most client questions during the 1990s were about how we select stocks – our buy criteria. Rarely did a question come up about sell strategy. In fact, clients often questioned and were critical when we sold to take profits and reduce overweight positions in stocks that were performing well.

Risk and buy/sell strategies are two very important conversations to have with any manager you use. And whether you work with someone or mange your investments on your own, the place to start is with a Personal Investment Policy.

Your Personal Investment Policy (also called Investment Policy Statement) is critical because it provides the guidelines for how the account or accounts are to be managed, helps set realistic performance expectations, and makes sure both you and your manager start out on the same page. Our firm uses a questionnaire to probe for the real level of comfort with risk – not just what the client says. Our objective form asks clients to select the mix of stocks to bonds they think most suits their long- and short-term goals. But a Personal Investment Policy goes even further. It identifies not only the mix of stocks to bonds, but also the strategies that will be used, the broad categories – equities or bonds versus metal funds, for example.

Most important for you is that a Personal Investment Policy states how performance will be measured and against which benchmarks. Comparing your portfolio's performance against the Dow when you have mostly NASDAQ-type tech stocks is no more appropriate than comparing large cap U.S. stocks against international small cap. Different asset classes will perform differently during the same time periods. One client reminded me that the municipal bond portfolio he was managing was outperforming the stock portfolio we were managing. True, but one would not have expected apples to taste, feel, and look the same as oranges. One of the reasons to be sure you are measuring against the appropriate benchmark is that it helps to keep your expectations for performance realistic.

How to be a Savvy Investor

Building a successful financial portfolio requires more than capable advisors; recognizing when and how to invest is equally important. Generally, savvy investors have certain traits in common and have learned how to handle markets in all their variety:

A great investor understands risk.

A great investor has a plan, is disciplined, does not get caught up in either irrational exuberance on the upside or irrational panic on the downside. A great investor does not allow his or her decisions to be ruled by emotions. By clearly understanding the potential for loss, they can allocate their funds among long-term, mid-term, and short-term money. With longer horizons before the funds are needed, a higher portion can be allocated to equities. With short-term money, the options are far fewer and are primarily money markets, short Treasuries, and low-duration bond funds.

There are no risk-free investments. Often clients move to what they perceive as low risk only to incur a higher risk than anticipated. Moving from stocks to bonds as the recession ends and recovery begins is an example. Buying stocks at the beginning of 2002 might actually subject a long-term investor to less risk than buying bonds at the same period.

Risk is also subjective. One client who started his own business nine years ago understands and is comfortable with risk. When he asks if this is the right time to shift the

40 percent in bonds of his 60/40 portfolio to equities, and I determine that he has a long-term perspective, I might answer that it looks like a good time to invest despite the choppy markets ahead. On the other hand, another individual posing the same question might receive a very different answer. Based on my knowledge of his situation and level of comfort with risk, I might suggest he mitigate risk by investing 10 percent a month over the next four months.

Understanding risk is essential to developing an investment strategy that works and produces repeatable performance over time, but it's only part of the equation. As individuals, we need to be aware of the times we are irrational in our thinking about investing.

Wise investors understand how emotions influence investment decisions.

The field of behavioral finance gives us some good insights into the most common mistakes people make and how to avoid them. While there are many, the two that might sound most familiar are:

Hindsight bias

In retrospect, it always seems as if we should have known just when the market would tumble or soar. Hindsight is always 20/20, and while it seems so obvious as we look back on the market's action, the fact is it is not obvious at the time in reference. Looking back on a particular time is very different from experiencing it in the first place. At the time of experience we are bombarded by a whole variety of data, which we evaluate to make our decision: Should I buy? Should I sell? At the moment of retrospect, though, all of that extraneous data is gone, and the only thing left is what happened. Thus we are struck by how obvious that seems.

When clients express that they (or we) should have seen the recession or the uptick coming, I respond that we all operate with the best information we have at any moment. The decisions we made were probably the right ones at that point, given what we knew. A good example of hindsight bias is most people's response to the picture of Bill Gates and the Microsoft crew in 1978 that comes up from time to time on the Internet. They looked like a bunch of young hippies, and if someone had asked if you'd invest in their company, you most likely would have said, "No way!"

Anchoring

I hear this type of thinking from clients often. Let's say you buy a stock at 80, and it declines to 50, and you think, "I'm so frustrated, I know it's coming back. When it hits 80 again, I'm selling." Or that hesitation about selling: You've probably experienced times when the stock you just sold rallies right after you've sold it. Now suppose you've been watching a stock, and it goes up and continues upward until you finally decide to buy. We know what happens next. In anchoring, we tend to get stuck on a number or set of numbers, even though many other factors influencing the stock have changed.

It's clear that as individuals sometimes our emotional responses get in the way of our logic when it comes to making investment decisions.

Confident investors deal with information overload.

While it is important to stay current, gathering too much information can lead to information overload – and the analysis paralysis that follows. It is important to filter out unnecessary information and focus on what is most relevant for you. Define your investment strategy and be consistent in implementing it. If you listen to financial news statements or surf the Net extensively, you'll have a new stock idea every 10 minutes. Don't allow yourself to become distracted.

Suppose you do all of the analysis on a stock or investment to make a buy or sell decision, and then you begin to second-guess yourself. Being successful takes more than analysis. It also takes intuition and steadfastness, rational thought, and the ability to put emotions aside.

Harry R. Tyler, Tyler Wealth Counselors, Inc.,
President and Chief Executive Officer

Understanding the Power of Compound Interest and Tax Deferral

We are told Albert Einstein called compound interest the "Eighth Wonder of the World." What he was referring to was the incredible power of compound interest over long periods of time. An easy tool financial advisors and educators use to demonstrate this power is the so-called "Rule of 72." For example, if you want to know how many years it takes for $100,000 to double at an average growth rate of 8 percent annually, simply divide the growth rate (8 percent) into the number 72 to get the answer, which of course is 9, or more accurately 9 years. If you are 33, expecting to retire at the age of 60 with $100,000 in your 401(k) plan earning 8 percent, you should have $800,000 in your account by age 60 with no additional contributions. We know this because 72 divided by 8 equals 9, giving you 27 years, or three "doubling" periods before age 60. In nine years, or at age 42, your $100,000 becomes $200,000, and at age 51, your account grows to $400,000, and in the final nine years, it increases to $800,000 at age 60.

Still another wealthy individual, J.D Rockefeller, is alleged to have said, "The best way to create real wealth is to never pay taxes on income you do not intend to spend." If you are accumulating assets or wealth for long-term financial security or an early retirement, then in general you will want to avoid paying taxes on the earnings or growth on your account or assets until you are ready to turn your capital accumulation into an income source. In the meantime, you will achieve maximum or higher compound growth rates if you do not have to take out money for taxes every year.

Simple Funding Strategies That Get You Big Results

If we can agree that tax-deferred growth produces greater and faster results than earnings or growth that is taxable, then let us explore some simple funding strategies that work. Unless you are already financially independent or retired, almost everyone has some amount of earned income and, therefore, is eligible for a government-subsidized retirement or savings account. This could be as modest as a $2,000 annual IRA or ROTH IRA contribution or as substantial as a $35,000 (or greater) annual contribution for a self-employed individual or owner of a closely held and profitable business enterprise. Assuming you are eligible to contribute $10,000 annually from your $150,000 salary to an employer-sponsored retirement plan, you will save at least $2,800 (28 percent marginal bracket) in taxes annually. Assuming your account value grows at an average rate of 8 percent, you will accumulate $908,448 toward your retirement nest egg in 27 years.

The whole idea is to "pay yourself first," and tax-deductible and tax-deferred, employer-sponsored retirement savings plans are simply the easiest and best ways to start. If both spouses work for employers who sponsor tax-deferred plans, they should both attempt to "max out" the contribution amounts allowed by the plan or IRS rules. If one spouse's employer offers a more favorable plan, such as greater contribution limits or higher employer matching contributions, then that spouse should consider maxing out, and the couple could reduce their spending or depend more on the other spouse's income for living expenses. Everyone's situation is unique, but the goal is always the same.

One common mistake employees make is limiting their contribution level to the employer's match level. If the plan otherwise allows you to contribute 15 percent, and you can afford this, consider maxing out your tax-deferred and tax-deductible contribution, whether your employer matches zero or 100 percent of your contribution. Consider the employer's matching contribution, if any, "icing on the cake," but never the real long-term benefit to your participating at the highest level you can afford.

Decoding Modern Portfolio Theory: It Can Improve Your Performance

In our investment advisory and portfolio management activities, we base asset allocation recommendations on the principles of modern portfolio theory as defined by Nobel Laureates Dr. Harry Markowitz and Dr. William Sharpe. The research of these two brilliant economists changed the standards for portfolio construction and has been the single most important influence on the practice of asset allocation in the past decade.

Quite simply, Modern Portfolio Theory holds that the whole is greater than the sum of its parts, and constructing portfolios using different classes or types of assets that historically demonstrate a negative correlation to each other produces portfolios with statistically higher total return potential and lower overall portfolio risk or volatility. Essentially, we're looking for different asset classes that, when combined in a portfolio, give us the desired return and risk potential and have "dissimilar price movement behavior," or tend not to go up or down at the same time, which enhances long-term performance.

In addition to diversifying through large stocks and smaller stocks, it's important to further diversify your large and small stock allocations between growth and value styles. Domestic mid-cap stocks and international stocks (both large and small value and growth) also need to be considered in the equity, or stock, portion of your allocation. It's also vital to include an appropriate allocation to bonds or "fixed income" assets, depending on the income beneficiary or owner's need for current income, as well as their risk tolerance and time horizon. Generally, the older you are, the greater your need for current income, and usually the lower your risk or volatility tolerance, which converts to a larger allocation to fixed-income asset classes. Historically, over long periods of time, stocks have greatly outperformed bonds; however, not all investors have the same amount of time available to them, which increases the role of bonds for older investors or those who just cannot tolerate great volatility or risk in their investment account. Modern portfolio theory devotees believe you should always invest for total return (current yield plus portfolio growth), since this ultimately drives the long-term performance of a portfolio.

As the following chart illustrates, the types of stocks a portfolio manager focuses on (their style) can have a profound impact on performance during different economic periods. This reinforces the importance of making sure both styles are represented in your stock portfolio.

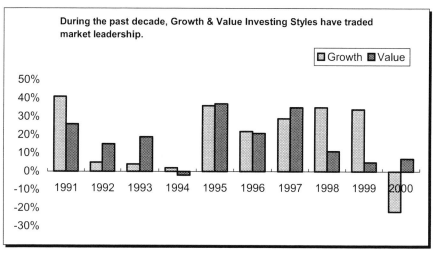

Source: Frank Russell Co.

Return Objective

To structure an appropriate saving and investing plan, investors need to consider what they want to accomplish with their money. For most people, retirement is the major goal, with college funding and charitable giving also high on the list. Once these goals and their respective amounts and timing are defined, and the expectations for inflation and the other portions of the IPS are decided upon, a realistic annual target rate of return can be determined. The emphasis must be on realism, for if the long-term return for the S&P 500 is 10.5 percent on an annualized basis, it would not be realistic to expect a long-term annual return of 15 percent for a portfolio.

Risk Tolerance

Everyone has a different level of risk tolerance. One of the most important things all investors need to have is a good understanding of the level of risk they are comfortable with, in both good times and bad, over the entire investment time horizon. In finance, risk is commonly defined as volatility of return. During the NASDAQ tech stock bubble of the late 1990s, many investors thought they liked risk (volatility), but they had only seen upside volatility. When the bubble broke, and they were exposed to downside risk, they learned that their risk tolerance – their ability to accept volatility in the returns from their portfolios – was not what they thought.

Time Horizon

Whether an investor needs the money in one year, five years, or 30 years will have an impact on the amount of risk they can afford to accept, what return objectives are realistic, and how their portfolios should be constructed. Many investors fall into the trap of focusing on the short term and fail to realize that when it comes to retirement funding, they generally have a very long time horizon. Many financial planners assume life expectancies for their clients of ages 90 to 95. That means if an investor is currently age 50, they have an investment time horizon of 40 to 45 years and will need their funds to last them for that period.

Liquidity Needs

The amount and timing of withdrawals from the portfolio should be determined in advance, as those needs will affect the structure of the portfolio and types of investments to be considered for inclusion. The liquidity needs of a 30-year-old investor who is saving for retirement and still working are vastly different from a 70-year-old retired investor who relies on regular income from his portfolio for financial support.

Tax Consequences

Different investors, different investments, and different investment accounts all receive different tax treatment. An investor's tax obligations can depend on the investor's current income tax bracket, the state they live in, and the tax credits or deductions the investor may have. Some investments, when held for a sufficient length of time, receive favorable capital gains treatment, while others deliver ordinary income taxed at the investor's marginal tax rate. Tax-deferred accounts, such as 401(k) accounts and traditional IRAs, allow investors to postpone taxes to some date in the future. Assets held in Roth IRAs can accumulate gains that are tax-free forever.

Christopher P. Parr, Financial Advantage, Inc., Officer and Principal

Learn to Avoid the Most Common Investment Mistakes

1. Swinging for the Fences

Many investors gravitate toward investments offering the highest potential returns while ignoring their associated risks. If your portfolio loses 50 percent of its value during a bear market, it will take a gain of 100 percent just to return to break-even status. A steady, consistent, conservative return will eventually lead to the accumulation of a $1 million nest egg. It is just as important not to lose 20 percent, 30 percent, 50 percent, or more of your portfolio along the way. This strategy may lack excitement, but will allow you to eventually reach your goal while sleeping comfortably at night. The goal of a well-diversified, balanced portfolio is to reduce market risk while earning a reasonable return.

2. Using Stocks to Meet Short-term Cash Needs

Funds that are absolutely required to be on hand to meet a specific need in less than three years – or more prudently five years – should not be invested in stocks or stock mutual funds. Examples of needs could be car replacement, the down payment on the purchase of a home, or even plans for a major vacation. The logic behind this is simple. Stocks are quite capable of losing 30 percent or more of their value in a rather short length of time. When these periods of volatility occur, the odds are that you will not escape the carnage. Based on historical data, it often takes two to four years to recover from a major market setback. When your goal is short-term, it is more important to protect your resources than to reach for higher returns.

3. Lack of Depth on the Bench

Diversification is the key to managing total portfolio risk and volatility. A portfolio containing primarily U.S. stocks will perform exceptionally well during bull market periods in the U.S., but will also carry significant exposure to downside U.S. market risk. Reallocating funds moderately between asset classes that have a low correlation to the U.S.

stock market can potentially reduce portfolio volatility without significantly sacrificing long-term portfolio returns.

4. *Keeping Most of Your Eggs in One Basket*

A concentrated investment strategy is the quickest way to accumulate wealth, as long as you make the correct investment decisions. It is also the quickest way to lose wealth if you make a poor investment choice. A general guideline is to limit any individual stock to 5 percent or less of the stock portion of your portfolio to achieve adequate diversification. An allocation above 5 percent is justified if you have a sound understanding of the unsystematic risk of the specific investment, including company and industry factors, and are confident that this particular investment can outperform the broad market or other alternatives.

5. *Tying up Too Much Capital in Low-Return Assets*

It is quite common for investors to gradually accumulate large sums of cash in low-return bank checking, savings, and money market accounts. Invest some of the excess cash or permanent cash portion of your portfolio in high-quality, short-term or low-duration bond funds with low expense ratios to enhance returns.

6. *Avoiding Paying the Government At All Costs*

Focusing on tax advantaged investments instead of after-tax returns. Investors often become obsessed with trying to avoid paying taxes. A tax-exempt investment must be analyzed on a case-by-case basis to determine whether it makes sense in a particular situation. The best way to do this is convert all returns to after-tax dollars. For the average investor, it may be possible to net more after tax by investing in a comparable taxable investment, rather than the tax-exempt investment.

Making tax reduction or avoidance the most important investment factor. The prudent financial advisor carefully articulated the recommendation that a young high-tech client liquidate one third of a $1.5 million position in highly appreciated stock of a single technology company. The stock represented 85 percent of the client's personal wealth. The client declined the advice on the grounds that the company was solid with a great future and that the sale of stock would trigger realizing a capital gains tax payment of 20 percent, or $100,000. Within six months and a major bear market, the $1.5 million had been reduced to $500,000. A million dollars in wealth evaporated virtually overnight! The only good news was, of course, that not a penny of it went to the government in the form of capital gains taxes.

Creating a tax-inefficient portfolio. A portfolio can be restructured to be more tax-efficient by holding the income-generating portion of the portfolio inside tax-deferred accounts, such as retirement plans. Also consider using a basket of individual stocks or tax-efficient mutual funds, such as index funds in taxable joint accounts.

7. Investing Based on Hot Tips and Rumors

Following this investment strategy is the quickest way to accumulate a shoe box portfolio. There are several problems with this approach, beginning with the reputation of the source of the advice. The second problem is that of placing individual security selection as the highest priority ahead of your personal goals, time horizon, tolerance for risk, and all the other critical investment factors that make up a personal investment policy statement.

8. Stretching for High Yield at the Expense of Quality

Income-oriented investors are frequently attracted to the promise of high-yielding investments. It is important to mention that investment returns have two components. One is the income, or yield, that is generated in the form of interest or dividends. The second is capital appreciation or depreciation (loss). Total return, the sum of these two factors, is the bottom line and all that counts. If an investment advertises a yield that seems too good to be true, it probably is. Yield means nothing if your entire principal is lost.

9. Taking More Risk Than Needed to Meet Your Goals

Do not take more risk than you need to take to meet your goals. This is without a doubt the most important piece of investment advice I have ever heard. As wealth increases, it becomes more important to protect what you have while earning a reasonable return, rather than focusing on achieving the greatest absolute return and taking excessive risk.

Clark M. Blackman, II, Post Oak Capital Advisors, L.P., Chief Investment Officer and Managing Director

Texas Chili and the Art of Investing: Shared Logic, Shared Rewards

You can equate the art of investing to the art of cooking. Any chemist will tell you cooking is a science. A gourmet will tell you cooking is an art. A chef takes ingredients that are known to interact in predictable ways, mixes them together, and in the end comes up with a creation that is mysteriously unique to that individual's skills and talents. Investing is similar in many respects. There are basic ingredients to investing that virtually everyone can agree on – cash, stocks, bonds, risk factors, and return expectations. However, a whole lot of other "ingredients" are required to make an investment strategy work for a particular person.

Let's look at Texas chili. Texans can all agree on some basic ingredients – meat, onions, chili powder, cumin, and peppers. But that's about where the agreement ends and the arguments begin. These arguments can revolve around the use of tomatoes, tomato sauce, jalapeños, habeñeros, cayenne, garlic, pork chunks, ground beef versus chopped beef – the list can go on for some time. In the investing world, this departure can be compared to adding hedge funds, options, leverage, or some other strategy to spice up a portfolio. Even when you agree on the ingredients that should go into the portfolio, like chili, personal taste dictates the amount to add. What will be too hot for one connoisseur is guaranteed to be too mild for another.

Like the science of cooking, the science of investing should be the basis upon which an investor makes fundamental decisions. Using proven principles, which are based on historic data and research, an investor can create a portfolio with *somewhat* predictable risk and return characteristics (it *is* investing after all, so there can never be absolutes in predicting outcomes). But there's a very personal element to creating an appropriate investment strategy that is necessary if you are to be happy with your long-term investment decisions. The need to sleep at night requires that the skillful blending of the right ingredients not be overlooked. That is the *art* of investing.

Marc Singer, Singer Xenos Wealth Management, Founding Principal

A Simple Investment Equation: Time, Money, Interest

There is the old story about one of the Rockefellers being asked how he became so wealthy. He recounted that as a child on the way to school, he would buy an apple for 5 cents. Once he arrived at school, he resold the apple for 10 cents. The next day, he bought two apples for 10 cents and resold them for 20 cents. This went on for many years until he slowly accumulated a small nest egg. After many years of saving and saving, his grandfather died and left him $100 million.

There is a lot of traditional thinking about becoming a millionaire, and there is also some outside-the-box thinking. The traditional approach is that you need to work very hard to earn a lot of money, or take excessive business risk in hopes of striking it rich. Of course, neither of these strategies works very well. From my experience as a financial advisor who has worked with hundreds of clients, the best route is the slow but sure way – remember the tortoise and hare story? In real life I have seen the tortoise win almost every time. So in this case "outside the box" might mean taking the slow but sure route. If you can reach your goal with 100 percent certainty, it doesn't make sense to take excessive risk by trying to get there a little faster.

How can $100 per month really turn into a million dollars? About 15 years ago I met with a potential client. The gentleman was a schoolteacher in the public school system. He had never earned more than $30,000 per year during his career. By saving about $100 per month since he was 25 years old, he had accumulated slightly more than $1 million, which today would be the equivalent of more than $2 million. He had invested this monthly amount in mutual funds only. Because of wise decisions, he never incurred any losses.

Actually, it is quite easy to develop your first million dollars. All you need are three key ingredients:

❑ Some extra money every week or month: About $25 per week will do.

❑ Time: About 40 years would be best – much less time if you can save more than $25 weekly.

❑ A simple and steady vehicle: I believe a mutual fund will almost always end up being the best choice.

When you mix all these ingredients together, you get the time value of money, also known as the compounding effect. Time values are very hard to estimate in your head; even professionals need a financial calculator. The trick here is to understand which of the three ingredients is the most important. Below is a chart showing how much money will accumulate over time if you save only $100 per month. Looking at the three variables of time, savings amount, and rate of return (interest rate), can you tell which is the most important?

Monthly Savings Amount = $ 100

Rate of Return (Interest Rate)

Yrs.	4.0%	5.0%	6.0%	7.0%	8.0%	9.0%	10.0%	11.0%	12.0%
10	14,725	15,528	16,388	17,308	18,295	19,351	20,484	21,700	23,004
15	24,609	26,729	29,082	31,696	34,604	37,841	41,447	45,469	49,958
20	36,677	41,103	46,204	52,093	58,902	66,789	75,937	86,564	98,926
25	51,413	59,551	69,299	81,007	95,103	112,112	132,683	157,613	187,885
30	69,405	83,226	100,452	121,997	149,036	183,074	226,049	280,452	349,496
35	91,373	113,609	142,471	180,105	229,388	294,178	379,664	492,830	643,096
40	118,196	152,602	199,149	262,481	349,101	468,132	632,408	860,013	1,176,477
45	150,947	202,644	275,599	379,259	527,454	740,488	1,048,250	1,494,841	2,145,469
50	190,936	266,865	378,719	544,807	793,173	1,166,910	1,732,439	2,592,406	3,905,834

As you can see, the rate of return is the most important factor by far. In the above chart, over 40 years, the difference between a typical CD interest rate of 4 percent and a rate of 12 percent is the difference between $118,000 and $1,176,000. In other words, 3 times the interest rate equals 10 times more money. This is a simple application of the concept of compounding. So to become a millionaire in 4 percent CDs over 40 years, you would have to save $846 per month. At 12 percent interest, you would only need to save $85 per month. This is probably the most salient concept in investing.

What are the best investment vehicles to achieve your goal? As I mentioned earlier, I have a very strong bias toward mutual funds. The rationale is very straightforward. Mutual funds are ideal for the investment strategy that involves adding a little money at a time. Much of the emotional decision-making involved in stock-picking is avoided. Introducing emotion into the art of investing is like smoking in a fireworks factory. It tends to blow up on you.

Give Us 5 Minutes, We'll Give You An Edge

Spend 5 minutes on the phone with one of our Business Editors and we can guarantee we will identify a way to give you or your company an edge, or find a more time efficient way to help you stay ahead of the curve on any business topic. For more information and ideas on how we can help you stay ahead of the curve, please call an Aspatore Business Editor at 1-866-Aspatore.

Call 1-866-Aspatore

Business Intelligence
Publications & Services

The C-Level Library

Empower yourself and your company with an expansive web-based library featuring hundreds of books, briefs and articles - all available in multiple formats - written by C-Level executives, and published by Aspatore. Available exclusively from Aspatore, The C-Level Library is the largest of its kind, and featuring the most extensive collection of C-Level content in the world, it is the ultimate reference tool. Such a resource enables you and your team to speak intelligently with anyone from any industry, on any topic. Every year, Aspatore publishes C-Level executives from over half the Global 500, the fastest-growing 250 private companies, MP/Chairs from over half the 250 largest law firms and consulting firms, and leading executives representing nearly every industry. Content is updated weekly and available for use in various formats - as-is online, printed, copied and pasted into a PDA, and even emailed directly to you. Another benefit of subscribing to The C-Level Library is access to an Aspatore Business Editor dedicated to your company, who can serve as an extension of your staff and help your team with any research needs. Drawing from all content within The C-Level Library, as well as the collected works of 30,000 other publications, including the products of every major business book, magazine, newspaper, journal, web and other publisher in the world, your Business Editor will deliver specialized services such as ExecEnablers^{TM} - packets of information to get up to speed for new deals, clients, projects, hires, and can even provide 24-hour deal research assistance. The C-Level Library enables you and your team to quickly get up to speed on a topic, understand key issues driving an industry, identify new ideas for business opportunities, and profit from the knowledge of the world's leading executives.

Titles in One Industry Only

i) Electronic access to publications in one specialty area (Select from: Technology, Legal, Entrepreneurial/Venture Capital, Marketing/Advertising/PR, Management/ Consulting, Health, Reference) (Via Password Protected Web Site)

Individual Pricing - $99 a month (1 Year Minimum)
Corporate Pricing - $499 a month (1 Year Minimum), $399 a month (2 Years Minimum), $249 a month (5 Year Minimum), Price includes up to 20 user seats (individuals that can access the site, both employees and customers), Each additional seat is $25 a month

Access to All Titles

ii) Electronic access to receive every publication published by Aspatore a year. Approximately 60-70 books a year and hundreds of other publications

Individual Pricing - $149 a month (1 Year Minimum)
Corporate Pricing - $999 a month (1 Year Minimum), $899 a month (2 Years Minimum), $699 a month (5 Year Minimum), Price includes up to 20 user seats (individuals that can access the site, both employees and customers), Each additional seat is $35 a month

Access to All Titles With Additional Navigation

iii) Same as ii, however all publications are arranged by different divisions of your company, each with its own web site. Upon order, you will receive an email from our editors about setting up a time to discuss navigation for your business.

Corporate Pricing - $1999 a month (1 Year Minimum), $1799 a month (2 Years Minimum), $1399 a month (5 Year Minimum), Price includes up to 20 overall user seats and up to 10 different web sites, Each additional seat is $45 a month

THE FOCUSBOOK ™ – YOUR CUSTOMIZED BOOK IN PRINT

Receive a custom book based on your Business Intelligence Profile, with content from all new books, essays and other publications by Aspatore from the quarter that fits your area of specialty. The content is from over 100 publications (books, essays, journals, briefs) on various industries, positions, and topics, available to you months before the general public. Each custom book ranges between 180-280. Up to 50 pages of text can be added in each book, enabling you to further customize the book for particular practice groups, teams, new hires or even clients. Put your company name on the front cover and give your books a title, if you like.

For Individuals $129 One Time, $99 a Quarter (1 Year Minimum) (Includes 1 Book a Quarter)

For Corporations and Multiple Books, Please call 1-866-Aspatore (277-2867) or Visit www.Aspatore.com for pricing

EXECENABLERS ™ – GET UP TO SPEED FAST!

ExecEnablers help you determine what to read so that you can get up to speed on a new topic fast, with the right books, magazines, web sites, and other publications (from over 30,000 business publishing sources). The 2-step process involves an approximately 30 minute phone call and then a report written by Aspatore Business Editors and mailed (or emailed) to you the following day (rush/same day options available-please call 1-866-Aspatore). Only $49 Perfect for new projects, deals, clients…

ASPATORE C-LEVEL RESEARCH ™

Aspatore Business Editors are available to help individuals, companies, and professionals in any industry perform research on a given topic on either a one-time or a consistent monthly basis. Aspatore Business Editors, with their deep industry expertise at getting access to the right information across every medium, can serve as an external librarian/researcher for all your research needs. Aspatore Business Editors can conduct in depth research and prepare a detailed report on any topic of interest (same day turnaround available). For more information, please call us at 1-866-Aspatore.

ESTABLISH YOUR OWN BUSINESS/REFERENCE LIBRARY ™

Work with Aspatore editors to identify 50-5,000 individual books from all publishers, and purchase them at special rates for a corporate or personal library. Employ Aspatore as an external librarian for all your research needs. For more information, please email store@aspatore.com or call us at 1-866-Aspatore.

PIA (PERSONAL INTELLIGENCE AGENT) ™ – CUSTOM READING LISTS

PIA Reports provide you, your company, or a division/group within it, with information on exactly where to find additional business intelligence from newly published books, articles, speeches, journals, magazines, web sites and over 30,000 other business intelligence sources (from every major business publisher in the world) that match your areas of interest. Each 8-10 page report features sections on the most important new books, articles, and speeches to read, descriptions of each, approximate reading times/ page counts, and information on the author and publication sources, so you can decide what you should read and how to spend your time most efficiently. Please call 1-866-Aspatore to speak with an Aspatore Business Editor to identify your areas of interest so the PIA Report can be customized specifically to your areas of interest.

For Individuals, $99 a Year for 4 Quarterly Reports, Copies Not Permitted

For 1 Report For Entire Company, $499 a Year for 4 Quarterly Reports, Copies Permitted (Reports arrive within two weeks of start of each quarter.)

For Multiple Reports For Same Company, Please call 1-866-Aspatore (277-2867)

THE C-LEVEL REVIEW ™

The C-Level Review is an essay based review that helps you maximize your strengths as a professional through the personal recommendations of leading C-Level executives (CEOs, CFOs, CTOs, CMOs, Partners, Lawyers (Chairs and MPs). Perfect for professionals of all levels and in all industries, the review takes one to three hours to complete, and you remain anonymous to the panel members, each of whom reviews your answers and provides a critical analysis of areas where you should focus your career efforts. Your results are compiled in a 10-20 page report, with separate reviews written by three C-level executives. The C-Level Review Panel, a highly prestigious group of authors published by Aspatore, includes C-Level executives from some of the world's largest and most respected companies. As they review your essay answers, they will identify ways to help you enhance your strengths, eliminate your weaknesses, and pinpoint where to focus your talents. Anonymous to both sides, the C-Level Review is an exceptional opportunity for professionals of all levels to get personalized, insider career guidance and recommendations from the world's most respected executives.

Only $499-Books are mailed within 3 days of purchase and can be completed in print-right in the book- or electronic format-in email or in Microsoft Word. Once the test is completed and mailed back to Aspatore, please allow 4-6 weeks for review to be mailed back.) Separate tests are available for management, consulting, technology, law, marketing, advertising, public relations, and entrepreneurship.

LICENSE CONTENT PUBLISHED BY ASPATORE

For information on licensing content published by Aspatore for a web site, corporate intranet, extranet, newsletter, direct mail, book or in another format, please email store@aspatore.com.

BULK ORDERS OF BOOKS & CHAPTER EXCERPTS

For information on bulk purchases of books or chapter excerpts (specific chapters within a book, bound as their own mini-book) or to develop your own book based on any content published by Aspatore, please email store@aspatore.com. For orders over 100 books or chapter excerpts, company logos and additional text can be added to the book. Use for sales and marketing, direct mail and trade show work.

Best Selling Books

(Also Available Individually At Your Local Bookstore)

MANAGEMENT/CONSULTING

Empower Profits –The Secrets to Cutting Costs & Making Money in ANY Economy
Building an Empire-The 10 Most Important Concepts to Focus a Business on the Way to Dominating the Business World
Leading CEOs-CEOs Reveal the Secrets to Leadership & Profiting in Any Economy
Leading Consultants - Industry Leaders Share Their Knowledge on the Art of Consulting
Recession Profiteers- How to Profit in a Recession & Wipe Out the Competition
Managing & Profiting in a Down Economy – Leading CEOs Reveal the Secrets to Increased Profits and Success in a Turbulent Economy
Leading Women-What It Takes to Succeed & Have It All in the 21st Century
Management & Leadership-How to Get There, Stay There, and Empower Others
Human Resources & Building a Winning Team-Retaining Employees & Leadership
Become a CEO-The Golden Rules to Rising the Ranks of Leadership
Leading Deal Makers-Leveraging Your Position and the Art of Deal Making
The Art of Deal Making-The Secrets to the Deal Making Process
Management Consulting Brainstormers – Question Blocks & Idea Worksheets

TECHNOLOGY

Leading CTOs-Leading CTOs Reveal the Secrets to the Art, Science & Future of Technology
Software Product Management-Managing Software Development from Idea to Development to Marketing to Sales
The Wireless Industry-Leading CEOs Share Their Knowledge on The Future of the Wireless Revolution
Know What the CTO Knows - The Tricks of the Trade and Ways for Anyone to Understand the Language of the Techies
Web 2.0 – The Future of the Internet and Technology Economy
The Semiconductor Industry-Leading CEOs Share Their Knowledge on the Future of Semiconductors
Techie Talk- The Tricks of the Trade and Ways to Develop, Implement and Capitalize on the Best Technologies in the World
Technology Brainstormers – Question Blocks & Idea Development Worksheets

VENTURE CAPITAL/ENTREPRENEURIAL

Term Sheets & Valuations-A Detailed Look at the Intricacies of Term Sheets & Valuations
Deal Terms- The Finer Points of Deal Structures, Valuations, Term Sheets, Stock Options and Getting Deals Done
Leading Deal Makers-Leveraging Your Position and the Art of Deal Making
The Art of Deal Making-The Secrets to the Deal Making Process
Hunting Venture Capital-Understanding the VC Process and Capturing an Investment
The Golden Rules of Venture Capitalists –Valuing Companies, Identifying Opportunities, Detecting Trends, Term Sheets and Valuations
Entrepreneurial Momentum- Gaining Traction for Businesses of All Sizes to Take the Step to the Next Level
The Entrepreneurial Problem Solver- Entrepreneurial Strategies for Identifying Opportunities in the Marketplace
Entrepreneurial Brainstormers – Question Blocks & Idea Development Worksheets

To Order or For Customized Suggestions From an Aspatore Business Editor, Please Call 1-866-Aspatore (277-2867) Or Visit www.Aspatore.com

To Order or For Customized Suggestions From an Aspatore Business Editor, Please Call 1-866-Aspatore (277-2867) Or Visit www.Aspatore.com

ASPATORE

C-Level Business Intelligence™